HOPE *is*

here to STAY

James,
Always keep
HOPE!
♡ Patrice Donnygh

For Lauren—I love you—Ampr

ISBN: 1-4392-3523-6
ISBN-13: 9781439235232

Visit www.booksurge.com to order additional copies.

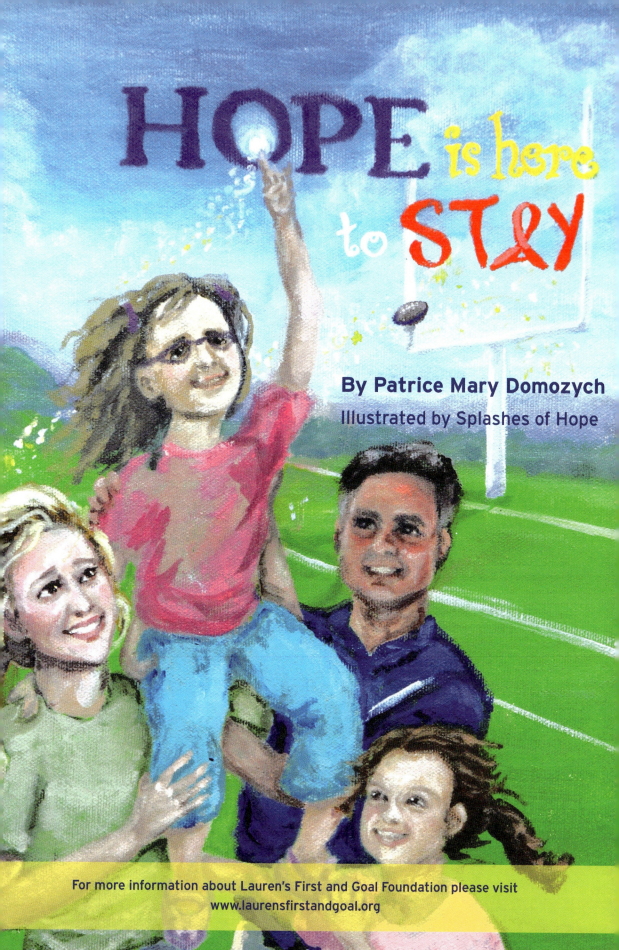

HOPE is here to STAY

By Patrice Mary Domozych

Illustrated by Splashes of Hope

For more information about Lauren's First and Goal Foundation please visit
www.laurensfirstandgoal.org

Acknowledgement

This story is one of hope. It is a story of finding something productive you can do, at a time when it seems there is **nothing** you can do. This book has been made possible by those who share this kind of hope.

The talented and giving artist volunteers of Splashes of Hope have been splashing color and comfort on hospital interiors since 1996. Frank Bandiero, Heather Buggée, Sarah Buggée, Stephanie Condra, Marie Doucette, Brian Fiedler, James Johansen, Andrew Silver, Beth Weiner Lipson, Liz Macchio, Sheauwei Pidd, Doug Reina, Leslie Sim and Frank Sofo are responsible for bringing this story to life in their incredible illustrations. Thank you for sharing Lauren's message of hope and for your dedication to this project. Go to www.splashesofhope.org for more information.

Thank you to those who make this story possible. You are the family, friends and strangers alike who join Lauren's Circle of Strength. You are the coaches, the players, the sponsors, and the volunteers who come out in the hundreds to take part in such a powerful effort.

It is said that the apple doesn't fall far from the tree. Lauren is a child with an amazing, resilient spirit who inspires those around her. Her parents, Marianne and John, live this example for Lauren and her sister Grace, demonstrating their own strength and courage.

This story starts with one
little child,
She's funny, exciting and
sometimes wild.
Lauren is a girl,
Like many in the world,
Almost nothing can steal
her smile.

You see Lauren wasn't
feeling so swell,
But she's so full of life,
you could hardly tell.

She lives for each day,

Sure to have fun and play,

And the doctors help her

to get well.

Doctors give her medicine and tests
   again and again,
They work to make her sickness come
   to an end.

Nurses so sweet,
Offer slushies and treats,
Make life fun, all those hospital friends.

Lauren, her sister,
her Mom and
her Dad,
See lots of sick
kids, some who
are sad.

They thought to
themselves,
What can we do
to help?
And designed a
plan that wasn't
half bad.

They pondered and wondered, imagined
and dreamed,
You see Lauren's Dad coaches a
football team,

He asked all his friends,
For time they could lend,
And at last they perfected their scheme.

They created Lauren's
First and Goal Football
Camp,

It was a crummy day; the
fields were all damp,
Boys and coaches came,
In the wind and the rain,
Each player left that night
a football champ.

All of the money they collected that day,
Would be counted and stashed safely away,

For kids who are sick,
So they can get better quick,
And everything would turn out okay.

What happened that day
was a wonderful thing,
Just imagine the hope all
those people could bring,
To sick boys and girls,
Like many in the world,
On one simple day in
the spring.

So here is the message

    Lauren wants to convey,

Each child can help

    another in his or

    her own way.

Use your head,

The news will spread,

To all the kids who
need some hope...
hope is here to stay.

HOPE is

Hope is Here to Stay is a true story about the dreams of Lauren Evelyn Loose, her Mom Marianne, her Dad John and her sister Grace to help others, like themselves, who are battling childhood cancer. Lauren has been living with a diagnosis of multiple brain and spinal cord tumors, Neurofibromatosis and Evan's Syndrome since 9 months of age. Despite all she has been through, Lauren is a happy, enthusiastic and optimistic child, with a crazy, infectious laugh and a true love for life. She takes great joy in helping others, finds treasure in what others may see as ordinary or mundane and never lets a day go by without some kind of exciting discovery. No matter what challenges are placed before her, she never gives up. Her courage, resiliency and relentless spirit are an inspiration to those who know her. Lauren lives with her family in Easton, Pennsylvania.

Lauren's First and Goal Foundation is a 501c3 charitable organization created to raise funds to support pediatric brain tumor research, support local pediatric cancer

here to STAY

services, to provide financial assistance to families living with a pediatric cancer diagnosis and to raise public awareness regarding pediatric brain tumors.

The fund is supported primarily by Lauren's First and Goal Football Camp, a non-contact, one day instructional clinic taught by experienced Division I, II, and III college coaches. Despite the rain, the first annual camp was a very successful day, with over 340 players, 55 coaches and over $20,000 raised for pediatric brain tumor research. The camp has grown tremendously since that first, rainy day in June.

It is our hope that through Lauren's example, we can help to improve the lives of other children and families dealing with pediatric cancer.

Go to www.laurensfirstandgoal.org

About the Author

Patrice Domozych is an educator who taught first and second grades for nine years. Since leaving full time teaching to be with her growing family, Patrice became an Adjunct Lecturer in Child Study at St. Joseph's College New York. Lauren Loose is Patrice's niece and goddaughter. Patrice lives in Oakdale, New York with her husband, Rich, and three sons, Thomas, Michael and James.

6969681R0

Made in the USA
Charleston, SC
04 January 2011